CRANE SONGS

Continuing Adventures of the King Street Girls and Boys Club

Written and illustrated
by Kevin Ernesto VanWicklin

Albuquerque
New Mexico
2018

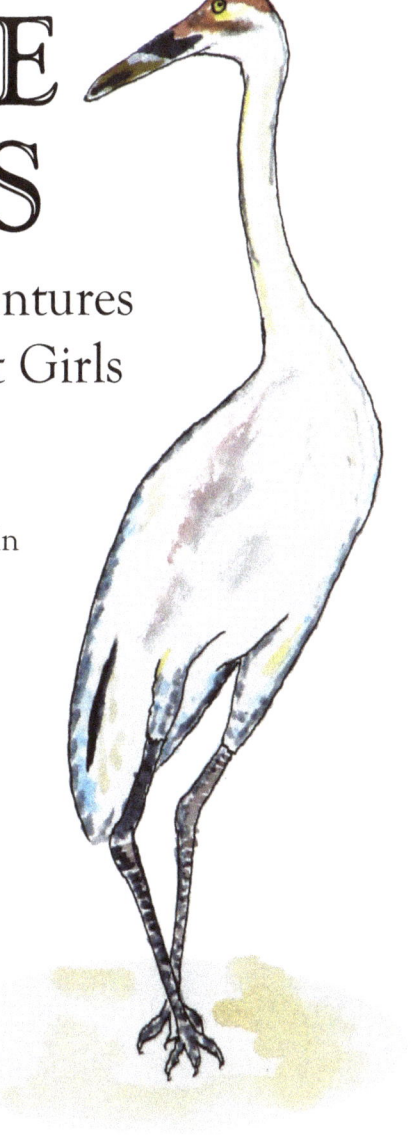

Crane Songs
Continuing Adventures
of the King Street Girls
and Boys Club

Written and Illustrated
by Kevin Ernesto
VanWicklin

Albuquerque, New
Mexico 2018

GoodFunBooks.com

Go to the website for
background information
and related activities.

Book design:
Kenesson Design, Inc.

© 2018 Kevin Ernesto
VanWicklin

All Rights Reserved

ISBN 978-0-9995591-3-0

This book is dedicated to all the cranes of the world and to all the people who care for them and love them.

Contents

1. Picking Ginseng 1
2. Feather from the Sky 5
3. Clubhouse Meeting 11
4. At the Zoo 15
5. A Letter to Baraboo 21
6. Crane Tracks in the Mud 27
7. More Treasure 33
8. Wild Bill's 41
9. Video Goes Viral 49
10. Whooping Crane Festival 57

Reflections of a Bird Lover
   A Story of How I Came
   to Love Birds 65

1
Picking Ginseng

Lin's family lived in Indiana for a few years. In the summer they made good money finding, harvesting and selling ginseng. Most folks thought that ginseng had died out years ago when the pickers exported so much to China where it was used as medicine. Well that was kind of true, but there was still ginseng around if you knew where to look and Lin's family did. They only dug enough ginseng root for this year and left plenty for future years. Smart. Good for nature, good for the wallet too!

In winter things were different. Lin's mother was a maid at a local motel and Lin's father worked at a store mostly cleaning and stocking shelves. He was never allowed to wait on customers or touch money. It wasn't much fun. All winter they thought of working outdoors again.

Maybe it was time to think of moving out west. There were lots of things to find in the woods and along the coast it didn't often freeze so they could work outdoors year round. Another good thing was there were more Asians out west. In Indiana everyone called them Chinese. They weren't from China and neither was their family. They were called other names too. It got more than a little old. Lin's family did move west. There was no ginseng but there were other things to collect like mushrooms and berries. There were even small rocks like agate and petrified wood that could be sold. Petrified wood are rocks that used to be trees. All the little cells got filled in with what was essentially agate. Sometimes they also found jasper which was pretty similar also. They even found some Elk antlers that could be ground up and sold as aphrodisiacs. Whatever that was.

Carlos thought Lin's family was really cool and super smart because they could collect all sorts of stuff from the woods

Chapter 1: Picking Ginseng

depending on the season. Carlos and his family went from farm to farm picking crops as they got ripe. Lin's family set up a nice camp in the woods. Carlos' people just made do, sometimes sleeping in a house or barn but nearly as often under a tarp with little protection from wind, rain, mosquitos, snakes or even from white men who would come in the night.

Carlos was very happy when his family settled down. His father got a job landscaping although sometimes he did miss moving around. When Lin asked him if he wanted to spend the summer exploring and collecting in the woods he couldn't say "YES" fast enough. Carlos was lucky his hands weren't needed to harvest farm goods. He would find his own way with his friend Lin.

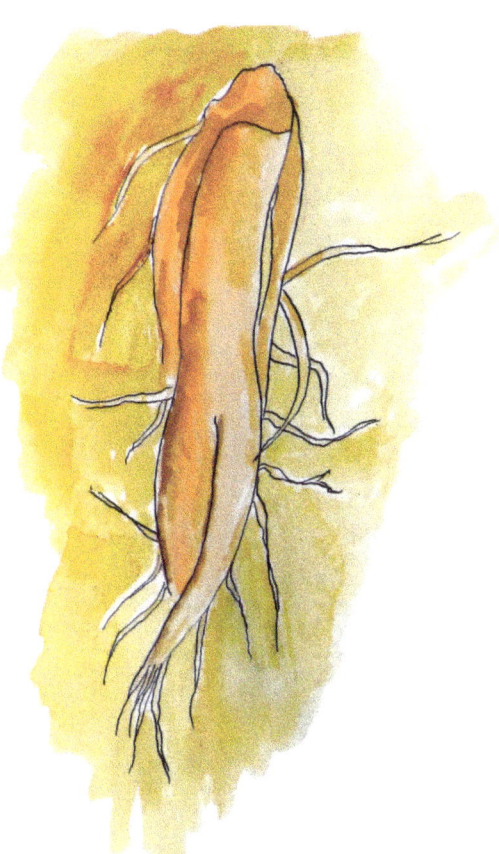

2
Feather from the Sky

While both Lin and Carlos knew their families were counting on them to make some money to help out the family, they also knew they wanted to look around and have some fun before they got to work. Neither of them looked at it as work but Lin's parents sure did, so the kids knew they should be at least somewhat serious. Carlos rode into the woods with Lin's family. Once there Lin's Dad told Carlos that he could sleep with Lin's brothers in their tent. There were only two in the tent and one more wouldn't matter. Everyone in Lin's family knew how to share.

Once all that was decided, Lin and Carlos made some sandwiches and packed some water for the day. They set off on a hike to get an idea of the whole area. The rest of Lin's family were already at work gathering agates and petrified wood from along the river. While walking in the woods the kids saw that there were many small strawberries growing in the wild. You couldn't make it a meal but they made a great snack.

Carlos, "Those are the smallest fruit I've ever picked."

Lin, "You can't pick enough to sell but they sure taste great!"

Carlos, "True that!"

Chapter 2: Feather from the Sky

Lin had found lots of feathers over the years. She and Carlos heard birds flying overhead. At just about the same time they saw a feather drift down by Lin's feet.

Carlos, "Look at that. It's huge. It looks like a primary wing feather."

Lin had no idea what that meant but Carlos did. His family often had a few chickens around and clipped the ends of their wing feathers so they would not fly away.

Lin, "I wonder if that feather could be worth money."

Carlos, "I know you can't sell Eagle feathers but I don't think that is what this is."

Lin, "Let's find some more."

Carlos, "That would be great! Maybe we can figure out what kind of bird it came from. Sunday my parents want me home to go to church, afterward we could meet up with the rest of the kids at the clubhouse."

Lin, "Sure why not! Someone there might know what kind of bird feather this is."

Carlos, "Maybe Omar, he seems to know everything."

Lin, "Don't count out Chloe, her people really do know most everything about the natural world."

Although they were enjoying exploring they could hardly wait to see their friends and show them the special feather. They still had work to do and for the rest of the week worked side by side with Lin's family along the riverbank picking agate and petrified wood. That was fun too. It was like treasure hunting, they were getting something for nothing.

Chapter 2: Feather from the Sky

3
Clubhouse Meeting

Come Sunday, Lin and Carlos were back at the clubhouse of the King Street Girls and Boys Club. They couldn't help but think of all the good times they had there, planning the parade and making signs, voting Randy into the club, carving pumpkins, and making Indian baskets. But also just hanging out, tossing cards into a hat and telling stories and jokes.

Omar, "Did you hear the one about the two boys who were walking in the woods and got lost?" Chloe, "No, tell us."

Omar, "Well there were these two boys named Shut Up and Trouble who were walking in the woods when they realized they were lost. Shut Up went to get help and ran into a policeman who asked him his name. 'Shut Up' the kid replied. The policeman said, 'Are you looking for trouble?' 'Yes' said Shut Up. 'How did you know?'"

The kids all laughed like crazy even though they had heard the joke a hundred times before. Some jokes never get old.

Today was a little different since the kids hadn't seen each other all week. Aside from being happy about being together again everybody had stories to tell and wanted to know what their friends had been doing. So far only Lin, Carlos, Chloe and Omar were there. The other kids would join them later.

Chloe, "I'm so jealous, I can't believe you get to hang out in the woods and treasure hunt."

Omar, "I bet you are making a lot of money too. I heard you were hunting for agates and petrified wood."

Carlos, "You don't know the half of it. We found real treasure. An exotic bird feather worth a thousand dollars."

Lin, "Well we really don't know that yet, we don't even know what kind of

Chapter 3: Clubhouse Meeting

bird it came from, let alone what it's worth."

Omar, "Oh it's worth plenty, I can just tell by looking."

Chloe, "I think I've heard of feathers like this but I'm not sure what it is."

Omar, "You know who would, my uncle who works at the zoo."

The kids agreed that was a good idea. They would leave the feather with Omar and head back to the woods. Chloe asked if she could come too. Of course they would have to ask their parents about that.

4
At the Zoo

Early the next week Omar went to see his uncle Saleem at the zoo. Saleem was working near the Lion exhibit. Over the heads of the Lions, Monkeys were swinging from a vine. Okay, not really, but who is telling this story? Omar's uncle was his Dad's brother and because he had no kids of his own he spent a lot of time with Omar and his family.

Saleem liked all animals. He had worked at a horse racetrack and then he had a job as a Veterinarian Assistant. When a job opened up at the zoo he jumped at the chance to be around so many different animals. Saleem didn't really have a favorite animal, although he wasn't very fond of snakes and other reptiles. It's not that he didn't think they were cool, it's just that he thought they were a little creepy and slimy and all that. Saleem later found out they weren't slimy at all. It just took getting to know them.

Omar was different, he was only so-so about animals. He had never had a pet and wasn't the kind of kid who would go around petting dogs and cats. Omar was a science guy. He wanted to know how everything worked. He liked problems he could solve. To him the feather was a riddle or problem to solve. He also had a small soft spot for birds. Of all animals it was birds he liked the best. Maybe it was the aerodynamic aspect that appealed to him. Omar loved to fly kites and one day he would own a drone that he liked to fly slowly. It was the movement not the speed that he was drawn to.

Omar, "Uncle Saleem what kind of feather is this?"

Saleem, "Maybe it's a California condor feather, they are huge. I guess it could also be from a turkey vulture. I just don't know for sure."

Omar, "Well if you don't, who would?"

Saleem, "Jasmine might, she's our bird expert."

Chapter 4: At the Zoo

Jasmine was also super cute and Saleem was happy to introduce her to Omar.

Saleem, "My nephew Omar and his friends found this feather. Do you know what kind of bird it's from?"

Jasmine, "It looks like a Whooping Crane feather but there are no Cranes around here."

Saleem, "How can we know for sure?"

Jasmine, "We could send it to the good people at the International Crane Foundation, they will know."

Saleem, "Cool, let's do that. By the way what are you doing for lunch?"

Jasmine, "Sorry I'm busy today. Maybe another time."

Saleem left wondering how it was possible to be sad and happy, excited and disappointed, all at the same time.

Chapter 4: At the Zoo

5
A Letter to Baraboo

Carlos was super happy to be back in the woods. He sure liked seeing his friends but all he could think about was treasure. He was sure the feather would bring more treasure. He liked picking agates and petrified wood along the river. Anything that wasn't in rows! Sure he had picked other things that weren't in rows like apples, peaches and watermelons. If you could call that picking, it was more like lifting. Some of those damn watermelons weighed more than he did. Maybe not really, but it sure felt like it. Carlos thought that was part of the reason his arms were so large. The girls seemed to like his arms. Carlos felt different. He was a bit embarrassed knowing how much work it took to get arms that big.

Meanwhile Randy was trying to figure out a way to join Chloe Quiet Dancer in the woods. Anyone with eyes to see could tell he was in love with her. Randy was coming up with a plan. If only the "Crane" would leave some tracks in the mud by the river, Randy could rush out to their camp with some Plaster of Paris and make casts of the tracks. He had done that in school and was sure he could impress Chloe with his plaster skills.

Mold making was pretty easy. You take a strip of cardboard and make a circle about six inches wide. You tape the ends, lay it around the track, fill it with wet plaster mix and, ta-da, you have an impression of the bird tracks. Oh, Chloe was gonna love this.

After Omar visited his Uncle Saleem and met Jasmine, who Omar also thought was cute and COOL, he went to the Post Office.

Chapter 5: A Letter to Baraboo

Omar, "I want a special envelope to mail a rare and valuable feather all the way to Wisconsin."

Postal Clerk Mike, "Who are you sending it to?"

Omar, "To the good folks at the International Crane Foundation in Baraboo."

Mike, "I've heard of Baraboo, that's where the Circus Museum is."

Omar, "I wouldn't know about that. Can I see the envelope?"

Mike, "This is our best padded envelope."

Omar, "That's what I want, the best. Thank you."

Omar paid for the envelope and postage and slipped in a note he had written.

Dear people at ICF,

My friends found this rare and valuable Whooping Crane feather. People have told us Whooping Cranes don't live here on the west coast, and that someone either dropped it or it's not a Whooping Crane feather. Please tell me if this is a Whooping Crane feather and how we can prove they live here.

Sincerely, Omar Ali

Chapter 5: A Letter to Baraboo

6
Crane Tracks in the Mud

Later that week Randy was still hoping to get out to the woods to join Chloe and the others. He had no idea that Chloe only went out for one day. Chloe's parents thought that Lin's family had enough kids to look after without one more. They also were thinking of maybe taking a weeklong family camping vacation. For now, they were keeping that idea to themselves.

Chloe sure had a good time on her day with Lin and Carlos. Chloe found an agate that looked like an eyeball. Soon so did Lin and then Carlos. It was kinda weird but the kids knew that these stones would be worth much more money than regular agates. They put these stones aside to go with the petrified wood that looked like a castle Lin had found earlier. It reminded Lin of ginseng where special shapes were worth more because people believed these shapes had power. You could call it magic. Shapes that looked like people felt kinda spooky, like witchcraft or Voodoo. The kids sure didn't want to mess with that!

Lin and Carlos realized that to find any bird tracks by the river they needed to forget about rock collecting and just search for tracks.

> Lin, "We are never gonna find any more feathers if all we do is look for stones."
>
> Carlos, "I agree, those agate eyeballs were cool, but they are not Crane feathers."
>
> Lin, "Let's face it. For now, we need to find tracks to prove that the Whooping Crane lives here."
>
> Carlos, "I know I sure can't afford a camera even if we saw a Crane."
>
> Lin, "We could maybe borrow a camera to take a photo of a Whooping Crane if we found the tracks first."

Chapter 6: Crane Tracks in the Mud

Carlos, "I think you are right, we need to find those tracks."

On Friday and Saturday Lin and Carlos walked up one side of the river and down the other. They went both upstream and downstream from camp.

Lin, "We walked a lot of miles."

Carlos, "I'm glad we did. I enjoyed it very much."

Lin, "So did I, but again we found no feathers or tracks."

Carlos, "I don't know what good it would do anyway. We don't even have a camera to prove we've seen the tracks."

Lin, "There might be another way. I just don't know what it is."

Carlos, "Me either. I'll think on it, maybe I can come up with something."

Carlos was clever. Lin hoped he could come up with a plan. She didn't know Randy already had the plan to make impressions in plaster of the tracks.

Chapter 6: Crane Tracks in the Mud

Not too far from camp, they did come upon the Crane tracks they were looking for.

Lin, "Carlos look!"

Carlos, "Crane tracks! I knew we would find them!"

Luckily tomorrow was Sunday and they could see their friends and tell them about what they had found. Tomorrow was close. As excited as Lin and Carlos were, it couldn't come soon enough.

7
More Treasure

Sunday found the kids at the clubhouse waiting for Carlos to show up. Not many of the kids went to church. Carlos sure did, his parents saw to that. Once Carlos showed up things got lively in a hurry.

Carlos, "Lin and I found the tracks we were looking for."

Lin, "Yep, right in the mud down by the river not far from where we found the feather."

Omar, "I heard back from the International Crane Foundation, they called me and said it was definitely a Whooping Crane feather."

Chloe Quiet Dancer, "Well now we know what we have. Let's prove it to everybody."

Carlos, "It sure would be nice if everyone could come out to the woods to join in the hunt."

Amelia, "I was going to save this for later, however now seems the right time. My parents agreed to take everyone in our camper again and Chloe's parents are also coming to help out."

The kids all let out a yell, "Hurray!"

There weren't a lot of reasons to make more plans. Just pack up and go.

Once they got camp set up the kids all wanted to go pick stones as well as look for the Whooping Crane. They had seen the castle stone and the agates that looked like eyeballs. This was going to be fun! Oh yeah, it sure was. At first nobody could find agates or petrified wood. Well Lin and Carlos could but no one else. All the rocks looked the same.

Sofia, "Is this an agate?"

Lin, "No, but I certainly can see why you thought it might be."

DeMarco, "This is a petrified rock, yes?"

Chapter 7: More Treasure

Carlos, "Sorry, no. Just keep looking."

Amelia, "How about this? Is it something?"

Carlos, "Yes, that's jasper. Almost as good as agate and worth something. Keep it."

Amelia, "Cool, let's keep looking."

DeMarco, "Of course we are going to keep looking. We are just getting started. I smell treasure here."

Sofia, "Me too."

Randy went off with Chloe to make the Plaster of Paris impressions of the Whooping Crane tracks.

Chloe, "Randy you are really good at this. Better than weaving baskets."

Randy, "I like this better. It's kinda like you capture part of the bird."

Chloe, "Capture?"

Randy, "I don't know. It's like a record that the Whooping Crane was here. Like a camera captures an image."

Chloe, "I get it, you're right. This is so cool. Thank you Randy. I'm really glad you are here."

Randy's face was turning red. He was embarrassed to hear such words from Chloe. He was super happy!

The impressions came out great. They washed a little dirt off them and took them back to camp. The kids all knew they had something. A feather and tracks. Take that all you non-believers!

There was a lot of talk that night around the campfire. Omar had brought some books and articles on Whooping Cranes. The kids learned all about how close to extinction the Whooping Crane had come. In the 1940s there were thought to be only 21 Whooping Cranes left. Through the efforts of the captive breeding program of the International Crane Foundation and many other people and agencies, the Whooping Crane was now doing much better. It was, however, still endangered.

>Omar, "Could you imagine how cool it would be to see a Whooping Crane?"

Chloe, "It would be better than cool. When you are given a gift in nature it gladdens your soul. It makes you feel whole and at one with the earth and all the creatures on it."

DeMarco, "Creatures?"

Chloe, "You know, animals."

Randy, "Are creatures like critters?"

Chloe, "I don't know if you are joking or not but I'm saying something serious here."

It seems like Randy was always showing off around Chloe. He might impress her more if he just acted like himself sometimes. He was a cool kid. He didn't need to show off.

The next morning found all the kids out hunting for agates and petrified wood all the while keeping a look out for the Whooping Crane.

Lin, "Remember to look up. Otherwise it could fly right past us without us even knowing."

The kids knew that. Still, a reminder didn't hurt. It's easy to get so caught up in treasure hunting that you forget about Cranes.

> Randy, "Chloe, I brought a gold pan with me. Do you want to pan for gold?"

> Chloe, "I don't know how. Would you show me?"

Would Randy show her? Duh, yeah!

> Randy, "I would be happy to. Let's go."

Chloe suggested they go up river away from the other kids where it would be quiet and they might see or at least hear the Whooping Crane.

> Chloe, "If you find gold what are you going to do with it?"

> Randy, "I would like to find enough to have a friendship ring made for you."

> Chloe, "That's really sweet. I'd wear your friendship ring."

Chapter 7: More Treasure

Was Randy happy? What do you think? They did find a little gold. Enough to make them want to try again. For now they needed to get back to camp and help fix dinner. They also wanted to hear how the other kids made out.

8
Wild Bill's

There was no reason to go to the clubhouse that week. All the kids of the King Street Girls and Boys Club were already together. What was even better, they were in the woods finding treasure!

Omar, "We need a plan."

DeMarco, "No offense buddy, but what's with the plans, aren't we having fun?"

Omar, "Sure we are. I just thought we wanted to tell everybody about the Whooping Crane."

Carlos, "How about we sell some of our treasure first?"

Lin, "I don't care so much about that. Let's think about the Cranes."

Sofia, "We haven't even seen a Whooping Crane. I say we sell some treasure."

Amelia, "I for one could use some money."

Carlos, "That's all I'm saying."

Omar, "I still care more about finding a Whooping Crane."

At the same moment Lin and Chloe said, "Me too!"

Chloe, "Jinx, you owe me a nickel."

DeMarco, "If we sold some treasure we could use the money to help our Crane. Maybe even buy a camera to film it."

Omar, "So it's 'our' Crane now?"

Chloe, "It's always been our Crane. With luck we can share her with everyone."

Omar, "She?"

Randy, "Him, her, does it really matter? Let's just agree we want to do everything we can for this Crane."

Chloe, "You surprise me sometimes Randy, you're alright."

The kids talked a little while longer. It was agreed that at the end of the week Carlos would sell some of the treasure at Wild Bill's Antiques and Collectables. While nobody wanted to go to town, everyone knew that Carlos would be in town on Sunday. They all knew why.

Meanwhile why not hunt some more treasure? As they were walking up the river the next day Spots let out a low growl. Amelia didn't know what to make of that, she had never heard that sound come out of Spots before.

Amelia, "Spots, what's up with you?"

Spots lifted his left front leg and held his tail straight out.

Amelia, "Look at Spots, he's posing for a photo!"

Carlos, "I think he's trying to tell you something."

Sofia, "Look!"

Chloe, "Our Crane!"

Lin and Chloe started hugging each other and dancing around.

Chloe. "I just knew we would find her."

Lin, "Me too!"

Chapter 8: Wild Bill's

While the kids were looking at the Whooping Crane, the Crane was watching the kids. She was walking away with long silent strides. A moment later her wings were spread and she was slowly running. A flap of her huge seven foot wingspan and she was airborne. Flying so fast and smooth. The kids could hardly believe what they were seeing. No bird flew like that. It barely needed to flap its wings to fly. What the kids didn't see because they were so busy watching the Crane, was that Amelia's Mom and Dad both had their smart phones out and were shooting video of the Whooping Crane. Now everyone would know that Whooping Cranes lived in the Pacific Northwest.

Treasure hunting was fun, yet finding rocks and stuff just wasn't as cool as finding a Whooping Crane in the wild. The kids all knew what they found with the Crane was worth more than rocks and stones. But how to cash in? How do you make money off a wild bird? They didn't really need to make money off the Crane, but they were treasure hunters after all. Wasn't making money the point? Maybe it was time to think about what they really wanted. The kids started seeing the Crane every day. They saw it along the river at dawn when the mist was rising off the river. They saw her eating strawberries out of "their patch." They saw it flying low in the evening looking for a place to roost. The Crane was in their thoughts and hearts all the time.

9
Video Goes Viral

Around the fire that night the kids talked about what they would do next. Lin's parents, the Lees, were going to go to town to sell some of their agates and petrified wood. They had quite a load, maybe a few hundred pounds. Lin and Carlos didn't have near that much. They did have their special shapes. On Monday Carlos and Mr. Lee went to Wild Bill's Antiques and Collectables. Wild Bill wasn't really wild that was just the name of his store. He was actually a cool old hippy who treated everybody right. Once you got past all the hair and the tie-dyed tee shirts he was a good guy to deal with. He paid good money. He could afford to because his customers liked him and were willing to pay plenty themselves.

Mr. Lee, "Billy, it's good to see you again."

Wild Bill, "It's good to see you also. Who is your friend?"

Mr. Lee, "This is Mr. Lopez's boy Carlos. He's been working with us this summer."

Wild Bill, "Pleased to meet you."

Carlos, "Mucho gusto."

Wild Bill, "Well what do you have for me today?"

Carlos, "I have some agates that look like eyeballs and a piece of petrified wood that looks like a castle."

Wild Bill, "Yeah those are nice, I'll give ten bucks a piece for them."

Carlos and Mr. Lee made a deal to sell the rest of their rocks also. They made out good. Mr. Lee then asked Carlos if there was anything else in town he wanted to do.

Carlos, "All the kids from the club agreed I should buy a video camera to take back to camp."

Chapter 9: Video Goes Viral

Mr. Lee, "Why do you need that? You already have track impressions and photos of your bird."

Carlos, "People are still saying that the Whooping Crane doesn't live here, that we used photos from Texas or Wisconsin. We aim to get a camera with GPS coordinates to prove where it was taken."

Mr. Lee, "I can't say I really understand what you are saying, but it seems you have it all figured out. Let's get that camera."

They then went to see Omar who found a camera on line that would be perfect. It was also motion activated so when the Crane came, the camera would go on automatically. Omar had it shipped to the park office close to where they were camping. A few days later the camera was set up near where they had found the Crane tracks.

    Chloe, "This will work great if the Crane is not scared of it."

    Randy, "We could cover over part of it with branches and grass to hide it."

    Chloe, "That's a great idea. How come you are so smart?"

    Randy, "Ah shucks, I'm not that smart."

All the kids were laughing, who says, "Ah shucks?"

The plan worked. Oh boy did it work! The next day the kids got up and watched the video feed on Amelia's Dad's tablet. There wasn't one Whooping Crane, there were four! The way each pair was rubbing each other's necks it looked like there might be more Whooping Cranes soon!

    DeMarco, "They really like each other."

    Sofia, "I really like them too."

    Amelia, "Yeah, who wouldn't?"

    Lin, "We should set this up as a live feed on the internet."

Chapter 9: Video Goes Viral

Omar, "I can do that."

Chloe, "This is going to go viral."

Carlos, "True that!"

Randy, "We are going to be famous for finding the Whooping Cranes."

There were so many viewers of the video feed that advertisers started paying the club members to place ads next to their video. The kids turned down some offers for dumb stuff like hair growth products for bald men. They gladly took the ad money for cool things like from a company that sold binoculars. Another company sold tents and camping stoves. There were many more offers.

The kids were super happy with all the money coming in, they were treasure hunters after all! Yet they wanted to do more to help the Cranes. People were already coming around the woods and getting too close to the Cranes and scaring them. These people needed some education.

DeMarco, "The money is nice, I've never seen so much."

Lin, "I know but it's not what we set out to do when we found that feather."

Chloe, "It seems like everybody wants to see the Whooping Cranes but if too many come, the Cranes will leave."

Randy, "Maybe we could have a Crane Festival and give limited tours. We could raise money to buy this land and protect it for the Cranes."

Amelia and Sofia, "Heck yeah!"

Sofia, "Jinx, you owe me a nickel!"

Spots, "Woof."

10
Whooping Crane Festival

Summer was ending and it was time to get ready for school. It was also a perfect time for a Whooping Crane Festival. The local paper The Harmony Times, which DeMarco delivered to customers, wrote an article about the festival. They also gave the club members free advertising space. Of course the kids could advertise on their video feed site also. Back at the clubhouse all the girls and boys were making plans for the festival and trying to figure out how to make it happen. Well that's what planning is.

Although the kids were happy about the idea of a preserve, they still had some misgivings. They couldn't help but think what else they could do with the money.

DeMarco, "I could buy a real nice Cadillac and my Dad could drive me around when he wasn't working and stuff."

Amelia, "I always wanted a pony!"

Carlos, "I would get a dirt bike and just go crazy!"

Omar, "I could get a really cool science lab with all the latest gadgets."

Chapter 10: Whooping Crane Festival 59

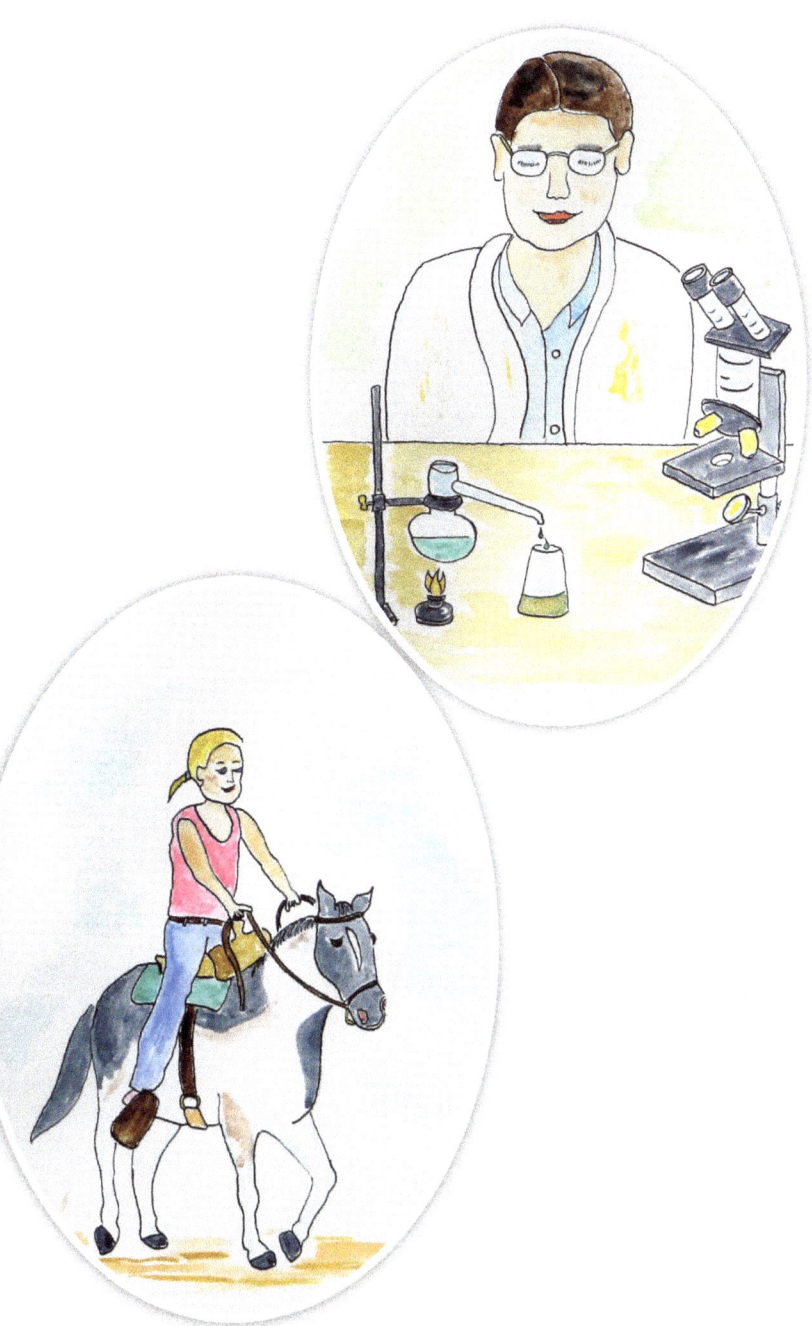

The school offered them the use of the playground and parking lot. They could set up tents for displays and stalls for people to sell tee shirts, posters, paintings, books, and all sorts of crane stuff. "Save the Whooping Crane" bumper stickers were a huge hit. There was talk that even the International Crane Foundation might come and set up a booth. The same was said about Audubon and the National Wildlife Society. Local groups would want to come too.

Things were really falling into place for the festival. One local rich lady heard about how the kids were going to try to buy the land the Cranes were on and get it protected for the birds. She offered to put up $15,000 and match any money the kids could raise. Once the local businesses saw the excitement they too offered donations. All those people coming to the festival would be good for business. Soon restaurants and motels had signs hanging from them saying, "Welcome to the Harmony Festival for the Whooping Cranes." Other signs said, "Harmony loves Whooping Cranes."

Chapter 10: Whooping Crane Festival

Not surprisingly the Festival was a huge success. Some people were kind of upset that there were no tours to see the Cranes. The King Street Girls and Boys Club had wanted to do tours, yet decided it would upset the Cranes too much. Nobody could have guessed what would happen on the last day of the festival. Right at noon when a lot of people were eating lunch from the food trucks they looked up at the sky and you know what they saw? Yeah, you do. They saw four Whooping Cranes flying overhead! It was a beautiful sight. Everybody had gotten to see the Cranes. A great cry rose from the crowd. A cry of joy! Whooping Cranes. "Can you believe it?" they asked each other. There was a lot of hugging and dancing all around. Harmony had always been a special place but now it was really something else.

The King Street Girls and Boys Club had the money they needed. Randy hoped the kids would forget about cars and motorcycles and just buy the land. For once Randy wasn't trying to impress Chloe.

Randy, "Let's buy the land. It's the right thing to do."

Chloe, "I hope all the club members feel that way."

Lin, "I do, it's what I wanted from the start."

Carlos, "Yeah me too. I'd like a dirt bike now, but I can find more agates and other treasure, I'll get my bike. Right now the Whooping Cranes need us more."

Amelia, Sofia, Demarco, and Omar, "We are all in. The money goes to the preserve."

The kids didn't have any problem buying the land. They were too young to own it but it was put in a trust. Now for ever and ever there would be a place for the Whooping Cranes.

Slowly things returned to normal. The Whooping Cranes left for the winter. No one was sure where they went or even when they went. One day they were just gone. All anyone could do was wait until next summer when it was sure they would come back. The kids had learned a lot. They found out they could help change

Chapter 10: Whooping Crane Festival

and protect their world and animals in it. They found they didn't need grownups to do everything for them. They had power! Maybe best of all they had found great treasure in the Whooping Crane. Who could have guessed how much money they could make from a bird with the video feed and festival? The whole town was proud of what the kids had done.

The kids are alright.

Reflections of a Bird Lover
A Story of How I Came to Love Birds

As a kid I endlessly hounded my parents for a pet, preferably a dog, monkey, or a parrot. That was not to be, instead I got a suicidal turtle who would roll over on his back and wait to be rescued. Then gerbils. They don't bite, right? Wrong! Not that I minded that much, but what do you do with a gerbil? That was pretty much the end of my pets, but not my love of animals.

We had a small woods near our house that had foxes and other animals in it. Foxes, I could hardly believe my luck. At the time they seemed very exotic, they still do.

An uncle had a gentlemen's farm where he kept a pony for my cousins. After the pony pooped one day my Uncle Max told me to grab some leaves and wipe the pony's butt. Did he think I was some dumb city kid just because I lived in Detroit? One day I would make a living as a horseman but no one could have known that then.

Later when I was around ten years old a pheasant slammed into our living room window. I quickly ran outside to find he had made his way around back between the garage and our neighbor's fence. I could hardly believe how beautiful he was. I knew my uncle and others hunted these birds. I also knew that would never be me. At this point my Dad came charging onto the scene scaring away the bird. First they shoot them, then they scare the injured away. Good lord, adults were stupid!

Having said that, both of my parents liked flight. In fact they were both pilots. I could fly also and I didn't need an airplane. Many nights I would lie in bed and dream I could fly, well, sort of. I would hold my arms out straight at my sides and let the wind get under my arms. It would lift me up into the lower branches of the maple tree in our front yard. As an adult I learned to soar parallel to the ground. Later I learned to fly above the tree tops. Many cultures believe that dreaming of flying means you will have good fortune or are simply very happy. In my case perhaps it was both.

One of my favorite places to go was Jack Miner Bird Sanctuary just over the border in Canada. Tens of thousands of Canada Geese would rise up from the fields at dawn and dusk. In smaller numbers I still get to see that at Bosque del Apache near my New Mexico home. This is the winter home of thousands of Sandhill Cranes and sometimes Whoopers! In fact a few short years ago my lovely girlfriend was driving my truck just south of the visitor center at Bosque when I saw three Whooping Cranes flying side by side only yards away. I've seen a lot of cool animals in the wild, grizzly bears, hundreds of bald eagles together, whales by the dozens, even a wolverine! Nothing, however, has ever given me a thrill like seeing my Whoopers!

But I'm jumping ahead. While still in my teens I moved to Montana to build a log cabin for hire less then a mile from Glacier National Park. There was a great blue heron couple nesting and raising their young on the property. Later the owner used the cabin to house a bulldozer operator who scraped the ground into a huge basin for a manmade lake. Good bye herons.

I bought a small farm in Montana. Many birds came around my place. Wild turkeys roosted in trees 15 feet off the ground. Daily I would see falcons, eagles, osprey and many other big winged birds. A trip to Central American let me view frigate birds. My time in Florida allowed me to observe anhingas, spoonbills, egrets, curlews and others. When I first saw a curlew in New Mexico while out birding with a professional biologist, I knew what I saw even if it was brown not white. I will admit I was plenty surprised to see a curlew in the desert, not on the beach!

Also while in Florida I made a new friend, a red lord amazon parrot named Bubba. Turns out he was a she. She went from trying to bite off my fingers to nibbling my ears while in the shower. Bubba loved her daily shower. She also loved to ride in the truck with the window down with never a thought of flying away.

I recently went to Tallulah, Louisiana to pursue my studies of the history of the ivory-billed woodpecker. No I didn't see one, and neither will you. I can say this with the utmost of certainty, without our help the whooping crane will go the way of the ivory-billed woodpecker and so many more species. The whooping cranes simply can't make it on their own at this point with so many people living in their historical habitat. But we can share the land and save the whooping crane. It's mostly a matter of will.

I've shared a story about the ivory-billed woodpecker on our website GoodFunBooks.com. You will see how close we were to saving this now extinct bird. Hopefully that will inspire you to join the effort to save our whooping cranes.

There are many bird and wildlife adventures ahead. Recently I saw what looked like seagulls next to a lake in Central New Mexico. As I got closer I was amazed at the size of the birds. These were no seagulls, but a flock of maybe twenty osprey. I've always thought of osprey as solitary birds, however, when migrating they travel together. This flock was also on the ground. I can't remember ever seeing osprey on the ground, they are always perched in trees or flying. Nature often surprises.

Kevin Ernesto VanWicklin
Albuquerque, New Mexico
Spring 2018

Photo from *Big Wings/Big Love*, a solo art exhibition by the author at the Randall Davey Audubon Center in Santa Fe, New Mexico.

Kevin Ernesto VanWicklin is an artist and author living in Albuquerque, New Mexico where he welcomes the annual migration of the cranes as they settle to winter in the area. He's had an avid interest in birds since a child and is a longtime member of The International Crane Foundation and the National Audubon Society. He believes everyone can support nature every day in their own way.

Crane Songs is the second book in his series recounting The Adventures of the King Street Girls and Boys Club. To learn more visit the website GoodFunBooks.com.

www.ingramcontent.com/pod-product-compliance
Lightning Source LLC
Chambersburg PA
CBHW051603010526
44118CB00023B/2798